Bamboo on the Tracks:

Sakura Snow and Colt Peacemaker

poems by

Tony Wallin-Sato

Finishing Line Press
Georgetown, Kentucky

Bamboo on the Tracks:

Sakura Snow and Colt Peacemaker

Copyright © 2024 by Tony Wallin-Sato
ISBN 979-8-88838-615-6 First Edition
All rights reserved under International and Pan-American Copyright Conventions. No part of this book may be reproduced in any manner whatsoever without written permission from the publisher, except in the case of brief quotations embodied in critical articles and reviews.

ACKNOWLEDGMENTS

"Alaska"; "Bastille Day 2017" appeared in *Exit 13 Magazine*
"Fatherly Advice"; "LWOP"; "Good Times" appeared in *Zaum 25*
"EVERYTHING IS KINDING, EVERYTHING BURNS" appeared in *Toyon Literary Journal*
"The First person I Remember Having Sex With" appeared in *RipRap*
"Low n Slow"; "Meditations on the Anti-Asian Spa Shooting"; My secretary is piled with prison letters"; appeared in *Yellow Medicine Review*
"Crestline"; "The Jade: Tenement Building"; "Junkie" appeared in *Anti-Heroin Chic*
"Marina" appeared in *The Paddock Review*
"Hotel Life" appeared in *Konch Magazine*
"In Seattle"; "Street Funeral" appeared in the chapbook *Hyouhakusha: Desolate Travels of a Junkie on the Road*

Publisher: Leah Huete de Maines
Editor: Christen Kincaid
Cover Art: Megumi Keleman
Author Photo: Lonnie Anderson
Cover Design: Elizabeth Maines McCleavy

Order online: www.finishinglinepress.com
also available on amazon.com

Author inquiries and mail orders:
Finishing Line Press
PO Box 1626
Georgetown, Kentucky 40324
USA

Contents

I. Shō 性

Elam Camp Backcountry Redwoods 1
Short of Language in a Day on the Rue 3
In Seattle 4
Alaska 6
Tehachapi, or Mountain Passes Passed Through the Night 7
In Kern County 9
Crestline 11
The Jade: Tenement Building 17
Bastille Day 2017 19
Spanish Harlem Food Truck 20
Certain Things 21
Street Funeral 22

II. Kū '空'

LWOP 27
Good Times 28
Bay Reflection 29
Psych Ward 30
Spanish Nights 33
First Questions 35
My secretary is piled with prison letters 42
Jack's Eternity 44
The First Person I Remember Having Sex With 48
On my birthday 49
EVERYTHING IS KINDLING, EVERYTHING BURNS 51
My Wife 52

III. Keitō 系統

Orizuru 57
Desktop Calendar 60
Hotel Life 62
Dislodged 64
Marina 65
Low n' Slow 66
Poem for Tony Gwynn 68
When I Visit My Mother 70
Junkie 71
When I Visit My Grandmother 72
Fatherly Advice 73
Meditations on the Anti-Asian Spa Shooting 74
Poem for Etheridge Knight 78

For my Okaasan and Obaachan...and especially my wife Audrey.

I. Shō 性

Elam Camp Backcountry Redwoods

We park a mile from the trailhead at sunrise
following the creek until the canopies sway left
the small town disappears into the pacific
as we enter the realm of huckleberries and *kodama*
        Charlie catches a toad two miles in
        penny sized and olive verdant
        blended like pastel within auburn needles
my mother says the toad is my spirit animal
(because I always lose fortune when I have it
and only appearing when I displease the spirit realm)
        in Japan *hikigaeru* represents good luck
        and should always have three legs
        when positioned atop a shrine—the tattoo on my elbow
only has two but she says *it's ok*
because it's better than my jailbird
ink—   Charlie places the cold-blooded vertebrate
        off the trail atop sunlit sword fern
        and I try to believe my mother
                whose tattoo of quan yin covering
                her shoulder acts as her own fortune collector

Orick Horse Trail incline switchbacks gravity
and swaying redwood branches shutter the shine
        hummingbirds flutter yellow sand verbenas and thistle
my old roommate is in the city wrestling
the bottle
        and a brand new baby full of hair
                his pack hung in the closet full of red dust
                        his face sinking with old age
        we yodel into the wind for him
        because his phone is off the hook & my mother says space never separates
she tells us to pray for him
and perform prostrations   I tell her he doesn't believe in that
        instead we wrestle elevation gain
        and down-sloped ridge loops—
                we chant the heart sutra in flatland
                because I heard it sung in a funeral once
                hoping the sentiment is translated

at the second summit alders appear
like young bamboo shoot groves
        my grandmother use to collect *yabu*
        for the fishing village roofs—telling

                              me *heavy rain is goddess crying*
                              when the salmon run is low—
Charlie leans his pack against the alder
to balance while he pisses on monkey flowers
                    I dig a hole and squat like my ancestors
halfway up the last peak I imagine
rescuing a young child from fire
weighing down my back like lead
                    Charlie relies on trekking poles
                    and small zig-zag struts
as a child my mother painted stories
        of Mt Fuji in times of depression
coiling on field trips to snow cap
            her details lead me to escape
my own Tokyo and explore
            the northern backcountry
every landscape I traverse
            I carry a piece of her with me

McArthur Creek Loop spits us out
where ice runoff flows gravel banks
                    Charlie collects drift wood and timber
                    while I set up tents and prayer flags
we use dry brush as kindling and spurt
bug spray to keep the mosquitos away
                        when my grandmother moved to California
                        she would steal aloe vera from Asilomar beach
                            because they were too poor for medicine
at midnight the big dipper is so prominent
I can see my mother's hand appear
grasping the ladle handle with shaky wrists
pouring hot broth in my time of sickness
                        the constellations sparkle like spices
                        grounded for healing the departed
                        and soothing the *swift-burning-flame-child*

somewhere *Izanami's* voice spreads across
the rice milk stretched above the dark canvas
blowing the spring current that carries us into sleep

Short of Language in a Day on the Rue

We emerged from the Trinité—d'Estienne d'Orves metro station
into an Algerian protest floating across the 9th arrondissement.
Sickle-moon banners and tortoise skin flags waved kindred
to schools of sawtooth eels and stale baguettes barricaded police
on roller skates. An Arabic-French mantra stuck to cobblestone imprints
like Edith Piaf's orphaned streetlight verses—I didn't know what they were chanting
but it was beautiful all the same—I thought of Jóse Revueltas as a child sitting
solitarily confined in a Mexican prison because his leftist dialect was untranslatable to
the government's hymn. We dissipated
from the crowd and fell into Picasso's apartment of paintings. A creaky staircase
spiraling into illness. Blue canvas stretched into naked gaunt corners.
The Tragedy spoke to me in brush strokes and madness. We never made
it to Versailles, but instead found flowers in between brick openings.
We took a swaying scaffold underground—onto an abandoned train track
that held weeds as beautiful as any Monet—from the left bank
we drank coffee and peeled oranges into the Seine,
drew nudes against cathedrals and spoke to gargoyles.
A swarm of bats followed us to Menilomontant
where we made love in a Keith Haring themed apartment in silence
because words were never meant to be spoken
in a room full of primary colors.

In Seattle

I can't tell the anarchists from the construction
                    workers, but I treat them all the same. Both
hold their part of the labor bargain and exit
                    from a job site we should all know. Are they
leading a movement or building one?

Capitol Hill manifests midnight vigil
across from a boarded-up precinct
                    I am enamored over the august expressions
                    in a sizzled state like lizards burning over an underpass fire
                    death is etched in the signature of the graffiti
                    memorial stretched across the corner liquor store—
                    operated by a man with an eye patch
                    and a store clerk with a short left stub
                            black combat boots
                                  nose piercings
                                      matted green shag
                            and construction hats
                        lean over flames
            that slowly wave
like half-mast POW flags.
        Today I am not on the offense/defense
                                    but stuck in observance.
The silent mourning strangles my priorities
and I'm inspired to visit Bruce Lee's
resting place.   *A compromise my wife would say*
                you can't be everywhere all the time.

My friend Jack delivered necessities
        for mutual aid this year in the midst
of rubber bullets and central valley heat
        that was never buried no matter
what the media tells us. Berkman warned
        us of the news.   I worry if Jack
remembers his medication—high doses
        for a mind that leans heavy on a gatepost—
When he calls me at 2 am I will have my answer,
        hoping he isn't sitting in the jailhouse psyche ward
for having an episode he cannot control.
        He's never been to Seattle
but I will describe it to him
        in my next letter.

A few miles west along the Sound

        an old fortune teller tells me ⅔ of farm
stalls in Pike Place we're operate by Japanese,
        after the internment there were none.
There *are* none

                Empty

Fog lights harbor the constellation drip
        across the Duwamish waterway,
the bridge is raised for
        a barge filled with merchant
marines in wool coats and short-billed caps.

                Absent

        Mt. Rainier resembles Mt. Fuji overlooking the valley.

The sidewalk wax-glow is transfused by shadows
        and I find myself on a northern island
        beyond the skyline, intimacy
        abandoned like soap suds spiraling down
        the bath drain and free range rabbits roam
        small grass patches along rocky shorelines
        and old town squares. An empty museum coughs.
Emerald fog separates spruce trunks from maples
        and hides the waning moon.
An independent bookstore
owner tells me his cousin
used to represent my district in politics.
        Voted out for incompetence he says.
His wife pops in from the back
        and recites a grocery list complete
        with cigarettes and kerosene. I enjoy
        her laugh. He asks if I'm visiting
        for political reasons or vacation.
I say neither and purchase
a book of poems from the first Indigenous
poet laureate before boarding a ferry
into the cold starless night.

Alaska

Along the Homer Spit, fishing boats sit on blocks. Boardwalks
on thin stilts, boarded for winter season. The last lines for Halibut

and Sockeye are reeled in from Kachemak Bay. The Salty Dawg saloon
is the only structure with an Open sign and a line of rubber boots and peppered

beards march in wearing orange and yellow vests. A bald eagle rests
atop patina rusted mast, swiveling its muscular head in search for shorebirds.

Locals will tell you *watch out for bald eagle shit when you're hiking the trail*,
as if common as pigeons parading Tompkins Square. Harbor seals

flip beneath waves of the western shore. The white tips of beluga whales
pierce the surface. Across the channel arctic blue glaciers, like transparent

neon signs, hover between the Chigmit Mountains and ice-tipped volcanoes.
They say *30-foot waves can generate within minutes from an explosion*

of Augustine. At the inlet bookstore, I strike up a conversation with a 40-year
resident. He limps in a cast fetching old hard bounds and travel memoirs.

Slipped on my last fishing expedition, he says. Piles of Alaska Native authors
line the entire first floor, wrapping around the poetry corner and ascending

the crooked stairs towards fiction. Athabaskan. Eskimo. Aleut. Tlingit.
California you say? Pretty bad fires this year. We talk about controlled

burns and the need for climate action. He is from the east coast—*came to Alaska
following a girl* he says. *Came to Homer escaping one.* A local enters to drop

off books and they both ask me why I'm here. T*o present on programs for formerly
incarcerated folks* I say. The owner in the boot leans over the counter. Breathes

on his glasses. Wipes the lenses dry. *My best friend is serving a life sentence
in California.* We exchange addresses. His, mine, and his friends, and I make

my way towards AK 1 heading to Kenai. A pair of female moose graze
bluejoint reed grass beneath the town's welcome sign.

Tehachapi, or Mountain Passes Passed Through the Night

Kory asks a woman outside the smoke shop
what's there to do in Tehachapi? We're on vacation.

Without a pause she laughs in our face,
lights a cigarette, and speeds off.

We get local stares as if we're sinking cargo
ships off the coastline. As if we're burning 50ft flags

stitched with stars. As if we're a palette
of blended paint—cracking the porcelain

into mosaic. This mountain town is the halfway
point to our final destination—another 14 hour drive

east but darkness is falling too soon for midsummer
and the train depot is silent. We are followed shopping

for camp food in Walmart. Pushed aside collecting
firewood at Savemart. Glared at in every parking lot

we pull over to rest in. The tight curved road to Tehachapi
Mountain presents smoke colored coyote. A litter just born.

Small ears like ripped flatbread not yet proportioned
to their skull. The headlights give no fear as they trot

through creek beds towards the fence-line of Norbertine
Monastery—bright red and deep blue stained glass center Jesus

on the cross. Colonizing the Creeping Sage and Deer Grass
shuddering the setting sun's fresnel lighting.

Tehachapi comes either from kawaiisu, meaning *hard climb,*
or derived from "tah-eechay-pah," meaning *Oak Flat with springs.*

Jesus was never here, never made the elevation gain
from Bakersfield, never replanted the native soil

turned over from Kaiju sized wind turbines. At midnight
we are alone atop the summit. Snapping branches

and sprinkling dry straw. Our fire is the only light
revealing the dust. The only sounds are crackling

howls rising from the low ground valley.

In Kern County

I met an old Japanese
couple fishing for trout.

They said they were from LA
but our shared resemblance
led to deeper inquiries.

Is it prejudice
for Asians to assume the ethnicities
of other Asians?

I didn't learn this skill
from my relatives
but from a Cambodian refugee.

> He was my boss
> while I worked at a bagel
> and bakery shop.
> He had every dialect perfected,
> from harsh Japanese pronunciations
> to back of the throat tongue snaps of Vietnamese.
>
> He was always performing
> impersonations while slicing bagels
> in front of a 5 ft golden fat buddha.
>
> His taro cake
> was the only delicacy
> I broke my non-dairy
> diet for. He acted
> as my laughing
> sutra guru.

The old couple were travelling
down river. I was wading north.
The evening sky shadowed twisted
Joshua Trees and removed the boat
reflections off lake Isabella.

*What type of bait
are you using?* I asked .
The old man smiled,

> *worms, of course,*

his short stubble creased,

exactly how Amy Ozeki
described crow's feet.
Or was it crone's?

                              I've been fishing a long time, no need to get fancy.

We stood at the fork of the Kern,
small rocks tunneling the current
to alleviate a still swimming hole.
I told them of my Hokkaido hair
and my history with Tokyo.
He told me *it had been a long*
time since stepping on the distant
shore. They pitched their line
and followed it until ripples
no longer sang a melody.

Crestline

雲の峰　いくつ崩れて　月の山

Kumo no mine
        Ikutsu kuzurete
Tsuki no yama

        The crests of the cloud
            Crumble frequently,
        The moon mountain.
            —Basho (1644-1694)

1.

On the way to my grandmother-in-laws property
my wife tells me of the time she took acid
as a teenager in Joshua tree—

winter break cactus wren, snow covered desert topsoil, an evaporation of self

"it wasn't the desert that made the trip turn" she says,
"but walking into a Baker's burger shack during the peak,
we waited in line behind a family of five where everyone
was bald and wearing the same clothes—I haven't eaten there since"

the dawning light refracted
through the soot covered windshield

                      spot-lighting her blue irises
                      like a coral reef Emperor Angelfish

her dimples pinched like a periwinkle
seashell

("eyes on the traffic" her repeating mantra,
the right side tires
        always vibrating on the yellow dotted lines)

as we transfer from the 62 to the 10 we hit civil twilight

and a western vignette of diffusion is only visible—incandescent
orange and cotton wool sapphire shaped like an almond
                      flutter above the pacific

shadows of sparse cactus and the city grid

become swallowed as we ascend the 18 serpent
corkscrew along the rim edge of the Transverse Ranges

a trucker once told me
"on the clearest of days you can see the pacific from up here"

he said this during the season
of iced-road car pile-ups

the only visibility
was the condensation
of breath hitting the pine

2.

The mountain town
of Crestline
sits 5,000 feet above   the San Bernardino Valley,
                                     named after the feast of
                                       St. Bernardine of Siena
                                       by Spanish colonists
                                       but really the land
                                       of Yuhaviatam
                                       "people of the pine"
                                       later given the name
                                       "Serrano's" or "mountain people"

the settlement is wedged
along the hilltop
in narrow windy slopes
leading to lake Gregory—leant
over frames, rustic shingles and shakes,
narrow 70-degree driveways

Top Town
Bear Claw Saloon
The Stockade—(where my wife's grandfather holds the record for most times being 86)
mile high backcountry antique goods and camping wear
                                       and a brewery that was once the town's library

my wife's grandmother bought the property
the year my wife was born—
ditching the congestion by the shoreline

for the A-frames balancing between
the Ponderosa and Black Tan Oak—
the bark covered in a million holes jabbed
by the red spotted woodpecker

during the chore run
she is followed
along the acreage
by an entourage of dogs—
Shadow, Queenie, Dexter, Trouble, Mystery, Nugget and the list goes on and on

the pig on the westside in the mud
never leaves the old camper shell—grieving the recent death of her pair Bam Bam the goat wanders
from horse stable to horse stable
bonking the aluminum
with maladroit hooves
and Betty silently chews
her feed, glowing cashmere fur

3.

The property is bordered by trailer parks and trail heads—
within the fence line are busted trailers
and meth heads—
some sweet and lonesome, others abusive and explosive
three tenants live in the pool room building—converted into apartments
but was once a thriving 1950s steakhouse frequented
by important members of government

> Jim lives with his small Ewok-like dog, always on his lap,
> a carton of cheap cigarettes and 12 pack of Busch,
> it's nearly impossible to escape conversation
> when you pass him on the property—either out of sadness
> or the tense isolation of living in the mountains

the other two tenants
are always arguing

over scattered junk
dispersed across
the westside corner
"I didn't steal your carburetor"
one screams
"I didn't take your dead mother's stuff"

the other refutes

        we are invisible
        to the quarrelling
        scene that echoes
        throughout
        the golden field
        canyon of rolling
        hilltops and bedrock

                blue Steller's jay wisp
                between the pine branches
                resting atop the oak stumps
                small coarse furred squirrels
                scurry chestnuts within vertical trunks

my wife first smoked weed
in the neighboring trailer park
when she was a teenager,
summers at grandmas
cleaning the stables
and feeding the horses—
slow gentle strokes
of long coffee patterned
snouts, whispering
Velvet Underground lyrics
to soothe their morning hunger
and clouds of 1 ¼ in. flies

        to see her dance between
        the stalls today is like watching
        embers burst from pine cones,
        handling the shovel like a vaudeville
        actress sliding across a redwood stage,
        her fingers gliding across the sheen

        coats of American Quarters, Warmbloods
        Tennessee Walkers and Appaloosas
        clicking of the back molars
        as if sounding the gong for morning
        meditation high in temple grounds

4.

Cedar wood chops like butter
the axe handle strikes through

like an open palm breaking
a river surface, cupping
a small fish and bringing
it into air

        black widows live in the wood shed
        but never bother flesh that enters,
        spiders are good luck in Japanese culture
        "if seen in the morning it's fortunate,
        but if seen at night be cautious"
        old superstitions I've heard
        from the elders of the land

when we visit
my routine is to chop
wood enough for the night
and morning, then repeat.
my wife sets up the a-frame
cabin—vacuuming and securing
any hole large enough for critters
to enter unexpected

        when night falls
                the summit is silent

        between the spruce
        stars are scattered
        like seeds, waiting
        for winter's clouds
        to bury them against
        the snowfall, we huddle

around the campfire
following the phases
of the moon rising
above the eastern ridgeline
and trace the newborn fox tracks
until we slowly drift away

The Jade: Tenement Building

> *The beauty of things must be that they end.*
> —Jack Kerouac, Tristessa

A mosaic of fire escapes
pattern crosshatch corners off 7th
giving weight to the old modernist
trope of neglecting the romanticism
of desolate bricks lined like a timing belt
        Carmen's figure half blended in shadow
        lighting a Pall Mall, sulfur expelling
                she whistles towards the greyhound bus station
                a swamp of men hacking over bent backs

the bullet glazed corner liquor store
blackened by guarded bars like claws
the residents all congregate to the graffiti line
damp brown bags scrunched in jaundice soiled ligaments
they cash their SSI and disability checks across the alley at Henrys
        single fluorescent saber lighting
        faces spotlit like bent shovels
                Larry slings nicklebags from the jukebox
                the vets hunt their reflection in the pint mug

the timeless tenement ghetto
is the plaza mayor for the noncompliant
red stilettos and white pearls knotted across knuckles
six flights of stairs stenched with sweat sex blood secrets
burnt carpet reveals fire survived wooden beams crackling bare trodden
        Lucas smoked in water while reading Hemingway
        too poor for a toaster, a razor never fails
                the candle wax stained the porcelain
                his cigar burnt down to his index and thumb

K St. below the rez hotel
buzzed like a Thai bazaar on Songkran
mermaid bartenders in tanks, karaoke joints, bright brass
downtown sparkled like a roaring nocturnal scene of Fitzgerald
but the flood of outdoor seated laughter stopped at the Jade's gate entrance
        Kiki strip-teased backroom specials
        2 am Coupe de Villes circling parking lot
                the rundown gentleman's club under
                moonlight, her fiancé away on tour

each floor contained umami
a unique flavor of downtrodden loners
dressed in drag, nudity or zip locked bags
French was spoken in whispers, plays enacted nightly
no one outside understood a miracle was performed behind brick
      Anthony was never given the right dose
      an imbalanced process of emotional recoil
            ostracized for killing a friend while playing with guns
            room 36 the only salvation into a neutral stupor

the train platform across the street
was mistaken for a departing breakaway
helicopter blades reflected the welding torch sentiment
obscuring the vinyl with 12-gauge shells and handcuffed violence hypodermic caps were
beacons like doorbells and hedges on the eastside
      I was young as a resident
      something I gained between Broadway and X St.
            the tenement fell to city planning
            like all great time pieces do

Bastille Day 2017

We arrive in Paris the morning after Bastille Day

a day after the 45th US president concocted a speech

backdropped to a French marching band rendition of Daft Punk

the anarchists question our presence

they say tattoos were no longer secret monikers

I learned in Spain to tell people we were from California

(even if it isn't true)

the Rue de Foch is barricaded by a bomb squad

but we have the pleasure to stomp atop masks resembling orange anuses

the Arc de Triomphe holds a socialist gathering for refugees

as if to personally tell us our country is failing the partnership

a film director questions me for ordering non-alcoholic beers at lunchtime

I invite him to the states to witness civil war for himself—he says he'd think about it

I buy a communist zine from teenagers looking for wine in the city park

one of them takes her top off and plucks daisies between the sidewalks

I follow a man I mistake for Camus—asking him how to deal with fascists

he tells me I don't need to use terror to write a decent play

as the sun sets behind the tower, we enter the Musee de l'Armee des Invalides

displays of resistance fill the hallways, revolution on a kettle mounted atop a pillar

Napoleon's tomb closed off to the public

outside a bride and groom dance like swans in the courtyard

and for a moment war exits my thoughts

Spanish Harlem Food Truck

I met her in front of a Halal food truck in Spanish Harlem.
The leaves were just beginning to turn green but cold
enough to wear ear muffs. When she smiled her tongue
peeled through the gaps. Her hands bore no wrinkles.
The man behind the counter knew her order.
This was her corner. An immigrant from Puerto Rico.
The same year my mother came here from across the Pacific.

Kids were throwing handballs against a tenement sized
mural. Bubble letters and purple popping. Large microphone
and yellow bandana. Her eyes gleamed when she saw the kids
playing. I thought about telling her I used to play handball
with a Puerto Rican in prison. I'm glad I didn't. Although
she expressed an indignant resonation for the current
climate. Her order was called softly. Small frame tiptoed

to reach chicken wings. She waited until my falafels
were wrapped in a warm pita. Never forget the red sauce
she said. We ate together standing adjacent to a skinny stoop.
Taxis threw hand signs. A beat cop flared his lights. A man
sold flowers to affluent couples across the street. A crescent
moon began to wane. My back pocket was stuffed with an old
French copy of Genet's *Miracle of the Rose*. She asked

me if I spoke French. I do not. Do you speak French?
I asked her. She did not. Too bad, I said.

There Are Certain Things

My father taught me. Like four cans of Busch Light
measures the inside of an AMPM big gulp for easy
transportation. Or owning a Nissan Xterra is the perfect
smuggling vehicle because of the hidden compartment
in the trunk. But there are other useful tools he taught
me, too. Like how to fix a rustic cabin breaker box
in the Tahoe National Forest at two in the morning.
Or how to escape a state unnoticed while in detox.
Trudging withdrawal cross country journey.

My father taught me it's never too late to reinforce
rebar across a broken bridge. And some bridges
will never have the stability to be crossed again.
In those situations you simply find another way
across. But that takes time. A concept he breaks
beyond in his moments of compulsive dis-order.
He once taught me how to send packages across
state lines through the mail without detection.
Or how to make the perfect breakfast scramble

by boiling your potatoes first, then frying them
in a pan. No matter how many meditation halls
or dragon temple retreats I participate in, my father
is the one who teaches me lessons on impermanence.
I recite precepts and sutras expounding universal
laws of guidance. But it is my American father
who teaches me the true complexities of human
nature and that everything changes, nothing
stays the same.

Street Funeral

I follow the skid marks and rumble strips
jump steel beams through boxcars adjacent to the LA River
REI tents tied and tethered to telephone wires
boarded noodle shops and 10 story buildings
        left to glass   parking lot fires
the mirrored skyline is overshadowed by the landfill everyone is living in
the block length concrete slabs spit venom
        into the graphite smeared above
a charcoal sketched Tabitha 7 shaped tail bounces from grated fire escape
onto New Orleans sunset Honda rested on bricks

graffiti tags that read "yo soy muerto"
        covers dented Industrial District signs—the sentiment
        is carried in third degree burns
        through gutters filled with orange caps
        surgical gloves   Bunsen burners
        dented Goya bean cans ripped on both sides
an outlined shadow mangled beneath a closed
warehouse garage door   a raven clutches a cigarette

an old friend is topless and does not recognize me
(it's been a decade since I've read Rimbaud on East 7th)
she spins across the four lanes with a four loko
a vibrant bouquet folded in a chair dragged with earnest
I count the shoes tied over the poles and lose track
        beneath a flock of warplane like pigeons

the 2020 world's fair balances on Main Street
        the boulevard festival explodes east into downtown Los Angeles
        but no one likes to acknowledge a foreign war on homeland
        city blocks full of storefront flower shops prepare
            for the noontime funeral
        the variety of petals appear violent contrasted
            with the motor city scene on the street
        streams of piñatas blow from exhaust
        18 wheels shifting between overfilled clinics

the hammer atop trash can lids echo from Union Station
        like a schizophrenic Wagner on Seroquel
I can taste the 5 am coffee at Denny's across on Alameda
        the only place to go after waking from the railyards
I hear the trains roll pass like a slingshot tin can ricochet

             desert sand mixes with sea salt   final solution of blood on the tracks an
abstraction of wrinkles exits the corner store market
tipping over his cane from a bottle of brandy
          across the street a woman silently waits
          for two cups of noodles to soften
          while she flutters with grace in her splintered ripped wheelchair

multi-colored new developed lofts perch on Spring Street
          like a peregrine falcon swift diving waterfowl
a family of four sleep huddled beneath lapis lazuli canvas
          attached to generator and 4 prong outlet
          they bathe in the yellow fire hydrant in secret
the Olvera Street cross depletes its magic
          security guards defy the saint's image
          and keep the road clear of basket carriers
Our Lady Queen of Angeles Catholic Church
          sits empty and starless
                    an old cigar faced woman throws rose petals
                    across the plaza and palm trees
                    tracing her steps with melted Mary candlewick

Little Tokyo is an illusion across from China Town's crumbling dragon
          old men kneeling atop mats light incense
          early morning cooks squat against milk crates
                    with Chinese cigarettes and Sapporo tall cans
at the end of the pagoda the imaginary border is chiseled like Pinturas negras
          San Pedro street reflects the aftermath of failed atomic fulmination
disintegrated projects ladle cadaverous soup in bowls that reach around alleyways
          the sequelae of landmines stretch swallowed into the horizon
          from 3rd to 6th I forget I am in LA—city of angels
          only ghosts reside amongst the macabre

in the midst of the Jean Genet play before me
          there is a shopping block encased by chain link fence
          high end highbrow nearly empty retail outlets
          designer wear and not a single imitation
          third wave coffee with organic beans
                    and imported sparkling tea
          those inside do not see over the wall
                    only their reflection from the downtown skyline
the flower district's corolla withers into alkaline
          a posey of orange marigolds flitter in the late morning tempest
                    the funeral is ready to begin

II. Kū '空'

LWOP

"Who's playing right now?" Mark asked on the cliff hugging
curves parallel to the pacific. I was too preoccupied by the power
of the saxophone lifting the sun to answer
Silence and stillness are sometimes the best response
Just like John Coltrane is necessary for 5 am drives to a prison
too far from anything

We parked in front of the Parolee Pickup sign
Three COs chatting away as if they weren't gatekeepers of torture
These are moments for small talk   piercing the cheek drawing blood with the canine
The female CO with the reputation asked where we were dropping him off
Mark told her Oakland
"I'll never go to Oakland, what a shit show" the CO said waving
her hands in a gesture like the mechanics of a guillotine
That's the problem with these people -- they use the word never in every sentence

We use to take the old chew spit from a CO and dry it out Rolling it in old bible paper
Using toilet paper to catch fire from the hotpot and carrying it to the bathroom
I thought of that CO waiting for the pickup and wondered what he was doing now
It's funny what one remembers when in the presence of guard towers and gun holsters

Mark's eyes watered like a child solving his first riddle
Eric's eyes watered like a child tasting ice cream for the first time
For 28 years Eric was denied the privilege of anything sweet
Today I saw the face of a man given back that freedom

Mark asked "how does it feel to be out?"
Eric counted the hawks he only saw from the other side of the fence
He hugged a redwood tree and stroked the soft fibrous bark
Before today this sort of act could get him sent to the hole
The prison defines compassion as contraband
Eric looked for the words like a search party out at sea

Good Times

I slid the syringe from her neck
like snipping thorns from a shrub rose.
Mahogany eyes rolling like a corner pocket
cutthroat shot. Her unfolding like the death
of spring. She smelled of camellias
her breath, lavender. I followed her iris'
to the place we all believe is real
a place behind head where altar flowers
wither in Billie Holiday lyrics.
A record player spun warped
in her girlfriend's bedroom

*"When I think of all the good times
that I've wasted having good times"*

but the girlfriend was long gone
blowing off steam from a recurring fight
that led her to me. Her floral pattern
spaghetti strap stuck to her butterscotch skin
like gift wrap slipping into the bent charred spoon.
Summer nights in the central valley offer no reprieve.
The fever damns impulse like a hungry tourniquet.
Her breathing resembled Cocteau's slender fingers
twirling charcoal above the playwright manuscript.
Folded over in reverie I remembered our childhood
together. Before our neck crevices were an open
woodland. Before we produced dandelions.
Before a vein meant more than humor.
Back when I didn't need to recall
her soft features like diamonds.
I choose to store this away
because it's all I have. She is gone now,
to a place I do not know where.
Maybe there are birds there, I know
she liked them when she was here.

Bay Reflection

I saw her face in the flight patterns
of geese. the bay receding, revealing
pockets of sloughs. Long beaks dagger
for purple dawn bugs. I thought I
would forget her in a county divided
by rivers and mountains, but she was
an earth sign, her body laid everywhere;
know-it-all, disciplined, self-control,
expecting, family and music. She would
say she was too complicated to describe
herself, you would have to work to know
her or keep moving. She had a figure like
Saturn: an orbital ring glowing, pulling
you closer. Cheekbones like Rihanna,
eyes like satellites. Who defines horoscopes?
Is it a mystical trick we attach traits to or do we
mimic what we read? The crab boats glide
between the jetty just before midnight.
The fog obscures the downtown harbor dock
from the northside estuary. A crescent sliver
pokes above the ridgeline. She would have
enjoyed the lack of light pollution and clear
milky way reflection across the bay.

Psych Ward

Jack called me from the Vallejo psych ward
repeating passages from the Tibetan book
                                        of living and dying

his voice a bull hide and leather strap
                                        coarse accents and short-wind

deep elocution of what I suspect Pushkin
                                        sounded like when reciting
                                              the bronze horseman

the great central valley
                his Petersburg
                                        psychiatric treatment centers
                                            his flood

I learned of Mischief Brew
Nietzsche and the Russian
revolution in Jack's section
8 public housing—how to hold
conversations til 5 am without
the use of amphetamines
or barbiturates—the importance
of combining rose hip
and lavender with cheap pipe
tobacco when poverty
digs the hole your creative
vices keep you above

he tells me he doesn't choose when he breaks
his mind fragile   tenuous splintered
                                          a mirrored reflection of Keats' physicality
                                          (I hope he is as loved when he dies too)

he read me a poem
about child molestation
        asked me to critique
                and to not hold back   there is nothing I can say
                                            to keep me from crying
                                            my only response
                                            is to *speak slower*

- - - - - - - - - -

the whole universe was trying to make me go crazy he tells me
transcendental meditation led to enlightenment   who am I to judge
                                                                         it was schizophrenia

psychiatry is forceful medication   as if offering sermon at Saint Peter's basilica
but jack is a bodhisattva   questioning *who am I saving if we are all one?*
Baudelaire said *get drunk and never pause for rest*
                                                                         or else we are slaves of time
Jack is in constant intoxication off thoughts
                                                               falling through holes out of sequence

I sometimes feel guiltyI taught him how to sit
and count his breaths   3/4-shut eyes 45-degree angle

I took him to a meeting once
in a new age hippie kind of store
we silently sat in the backroom   small perspirant circle   old wobbly chairs
he tells me that's where he learned to read minds

he entered hallucinations
searching for his ailment;
                                        dumpster diving Holstein cows
                                        dalmatians stretched manicured yards
                                        stranger's lock-jawed stares
                                        houses disappeared in a flash
                                                               only to reappear again

he doesn't tell me how he ended
up back in white cloth and brown
straps. The ambulance made it
quicker than the police—   sadly that's all I care about
                                        another stint in jail
                                        would have broken
                                        him like the parent
                                        of a purloined guerrilla
                                        trained child soldier
                                        lost in the jungle

a crow watches over him
          between here and there   then and now

circling deep blue stretches
        ripped open with cotton white
it follows him down Stockton Blvd.
        where he delivers medicine
to a friend's father who is sick   only, the father died a year ago

-    -   -   -   -   -   -   -   -   -

Jack tells the doctor he's a quack
the rebuttal is a 16-day hold
and 400 mgs of Seroquel

                tranquilizers and sedatives carry
                his Rasputin like figure through
                the window into San Pablo Bay

migrations depart
the national wildlife
refuge across levees

                he joins the red-tailed
                hawks and bright white—
                tailed kites over Tubbs
                Island—a peregrine
                falcon mistakes him
                for a shorebird stuck
                in the muddy marsh

pushing him further
and further into
the edge of the sanctuary

                when he wakes he is back
                in the pill container—conversing
                with a woman in a red draped cape

Spanish Nights

Lorca led me into a city
    made of hills that ended
        in a gothic cathedral,
            translated my weariness
                and confused outbursts
                      on pocket scrolls

and cobblestone,
    clay refracted white silk skirts
        that waved like crowning bell
            gables and sepia roman circuses,
                bladed weapons hung
                      in subterranean tombs

that unhinged along revolt
    made of religious inquisitions
        above the Tagus River bend,
            harboring synagogues
                oracular mosques
                      and shattered stained glass

I hawked eulogies composited
    behind 35 mm film suspended
        atop summer breasts, in a caliphal
            bathhouse I kissed my wife's small mole
                before unchaining her bracelet
                      and slipping off her boots

we roamed the mercado
    while the gypsy poet fell seduced
        by Wall Street, driftwood
            asylum camps like Harlem
                renaissance projects feathered
                      in dipped ink surrealist

counter clock images, street kids
    in Madrid stole my wife's
        journal looking for bread,
            she was upset because
                I invited them, I was upset because
                      I will never know if I am written

between the pages, naked
    bodies float off the coast
        of Valencia in the warm
            Mediterranean Sea, only old
                Italian men stretched like leather
                    on the shoreline as we let the sea

take us under, I saw my grandfather's
    stoicism across a bullfighter's face
        sitting alone with newspapers
            in a Barcelona alleyway—
                hands buried in ink
                    slowly disappearing—

pickpockets led us astray
    between kingdoms and railways
        militia occupied troops marched
            with sculptures through mortar
                and brick portals, their shadows tangoed
                    into the Jewish quarter midnight

I caught a glimpse of *paseo*
    egg shells scattered across
        confessionals and my wife peeled
            back the corners of the moon
                exposing a burnt-edged postcard
                    with an imprinted dream:

        the whole atmosphere has a certain finite tic, like the ash of a
        cigarette…and I wept beneath a pale glow of silence

First Questions

1.   *Wharf*
Ragdoll spiked pelican swooped
6ft wingspan open vacuum billed
flight. My brother, 7 years old,
holds hot dog at the end of the pier.
Lost sight of my mother, who sings
to me in the stroller to keep me
from crying. Cloudless boat docks
and headstone-still sails align across
Monterey bay. Tourists laugh
with ice cream cones dripping
through the wooden plank cracks
leading to the clam chowder
smoke of the Fisherman's grill.
Wide tanks of convicted crab
and lobsters, rubber bands hand
cuffed closed claws. Lazy Sunday
strides of fisherman, housewives,
out of town spectacles and graveyard
shift coast guard insomniacs. Ghost
canners of sardine canneries bend
around Lighthouse Ave and Lee Chong
slips credit to the misfortune band
of flophouse dwellers. The two
story tin roofed pinball wonderland
unravels their door, children flood
the antique carousel spinning clockwise,
up and down, up and down. The dark
spotted milk-white pelican swan dives
like a sunspot bleached against
the chalcedony blue overhead
and swallows whole my brother's
hotdog, who is lost in imagination
at the surf. Terrified screams
reverberates through the gift shops
and abalone warehouses—my crying
stops and I join the beached harbor
seals in the early morning laughter.

2.   Unsolved mysteries
My grandmother was passed
house to house when the hospital
held no room. Her north highlands

home off Karl St. encased with second
hand smoke. Yellow stained walls
and the once off-white popcorn
ceiling was no longer *off* anything
but a completely mahogany stained
surface. Lung cancer spread rapidly
through her frail skeleton frame, slightly
transparent beneath bright sunlight.
Two packs a day, an ember always
aflame, sneaking puffs behind
my auntie's garage door until
they no longer could take the sight
of death's hand coiling from below.
My brother left for college, granny
moved into the small bedroom I acquired
night terrors, and I quickly took up
the space down the hall. After school
I would find granny with her signature
32 oz unsweetened tea slumped
over the corner of the bed, her feet
2 in above the carpet. I would snuggle
with my snacks atop her lap
and get lost in reruns of unsolved
mysteries until I nodded
off into my afternoon nap.

3.	*White Walls*
Ponderosa and White fir covered
in opaque drift like dusty book
bindings. Aquatic sheen Western
Tanager squabbles adjacent
Yellow-Billed black bird nested
with pine sap and end of summer
charred birch bark. Tahoe
Basin envelops winter silence
across hidden trails ascending
towards Tallic and Pyramid
Peak. Our family huddles next
to the centered fireplace with hot
cocoa and hot toddies. Cinnamon
steam secretes from our cold
vice gripped fingers. The adults
are sober and us children are curled

atop monopoly board game money
and candy land pieces. Dice
and dominoes slam against the dining
room table, shaking the cabin wood
beams. Howls and creaks. The elders
are chemists in the kitchen swirling
cauldrons of boiling liquid waiting
to simmer. A winter storm crosses
state lines from Nevada the night before
we are supposed to leave. The front
door is blocked, the windows are walls
of fluff, the snow keeps us together
for one more night.

4.   *Sapphire*
Heaven lies off highway 80
between the lowland valley and
Sierra Nevada high elevation.
Lone marker signals blissful
paradise in form of emerald-hued
water flowing abundant: above,
under, through and over youthful
granite slab boulders. A mile trek
from the dust beneath forested grove
of pine and manzanita protruding
northern cliff sides, high noon refraction
leads you to an oasis detailed in ancient
fables and campfire myths. Southfork
Yuba glides like a vein waiting to be hit.
Glistened canyon deep drop waterfall.
Billy goat ledge steps hand grappled
swung rock wall. The plunge ice
capped hot summer days. Milky
way stretches thick like bracelet band
sapphire. The top of the 80ft jump caresses
homemade grave markers for the broken
ribbed past floating bodies. Incense
at midnight and tattered prayer flag
waves even on a windless night.

5.   *Postcards*
She sent a drawing colored in pencil
and pastel rainbows. I used the labels

from the travel pack deodorant
from commissary to hang the artwork
on the concrete behind my bunk.
Not many friends sent news
from the outside. Her message
detailed her struggle with committing
herself again for a reset. She was back
at work teaching the special needs
class at our old high school. I waited
a couple weeks to respond to the letter
because I was afraid she wouldn't
send one back. For those 21 days
I felt like someone on the other side
cared whether I was doing alright.

6.   *Tambourine Man*
I brought homemade moonshine
to a Dylan show. The concert
was held at the Oklahoma Fairgrounds.
A day time carnival kind of gig.
I made the liquor myself and added
grape flavoring. I don't recommend
following those steps. The California
court system sent me to the Midwest
instead of prison as a teenager. I imagined
I was going to follow the Guthrie trail.
I bought the concert tickets with the money
I earned working for a plant nursery.
I don't remember the opening act,
Except for a pretty face and shiny
guitar. When Dylan took the stage
with *Like a Rolling Stone,* an older
woman approached me with a bag
of mushrooms. We swapped poisons
and danced for what seemed like hours.
Everything went black and I woke
up at a gas station handcuffed
in mid-sentence with a sheriff's deputy.

7.   *Stones*
My second kidney surgery
ended in a disaster. The first
one left scar tissue that made

it difficult to operate on. I made
the mistake of telling the surgeon
I was allergic to opiates. They asked
how severe and I replied *I break
out in felonies and handcuffs.*
The comment didn't humor them
and they decided to only give
me ibuprofen after the procedure.
Audrey and my brother had to fight
to get me pain relief. The ride home
from San Francisco was like driving
over braille on a flat-tired pocket
bike. Weeks of amnesia and sweat
soaked sheets. Weeks of *On The Road*
listened to through Greg's tape recorder,
old and warped, read by Matt Dillon.
Weeks of curling into shapes we make
the 9 months before we are born. Weeks
of missed Halloween shows and festivals.
Weeks of fallen persimmons with no one
to pick them up. Weeks of pumpkins
carved, splattered, eaten and rotted. Weeks
of sober friends creating *what-if-scenarios*
and casting judgment calls towards
medication. Weeks of Audrey healing
me better and never leaving my side.

8.   *Twins*
He was on suicide watch the first
week of residence. Closely
monitored to keep whatever happened
out there from happening *in here.*
I was one week past two weeks spent
in the detox room. Conversing
with tacky wallpaper and vomiting
in a bucket that no one emptied.
I met him one night I couldn't sleep.
Pacing the patio staring at the cows
meant for positive rehabilitation efforts.
We spoke of heart aches and armed
robberies. Overdoses and silver
lined bullets spun in chambers.
Our mothers who never gave up

on us. We shared the same birthday.
Scorpios. Year of the horse. Our mother's
both worked for the same grocery store
and were born somewhere else.
We both lost someone unprepared,
and we administered the same numbing
potion. Group time circles of healing
and meetings of redemption. The presence
of counselors began to soothe me.
He never spoke to them. One night
I went to check on him. I found an empty
room and a note that said *I hope you
do better than me.*

9.	Hitchhiking

Late night cactus needle scatter
sky. State lines crisscrossed
sunsets sunken plateau bellies.
Red clay earth dust covering
dotted yellow dividers. Dylan
and I stopped for gas somewhere
between Barstow and Albuquerque.
Grey spotted Blue Heeler trotted
Over to the passenger side van
door. Mike followed close behind.
He was wearing a tie dyed bandana,
gingerbread vest and welcoming smile
set to the tune of some Grateful
Dead rhythm. Beneath moonlight
His charcoal stubble glinted dew
drops of sweat from the hot summer
night. *Can Sadie and I get a ride?*
We spoke of the Tao, music, protests
and war. Mike survived Vietnam
and dedicated his life to non-violence.
We dropped him and Sadie off
at the highway connection to Flagstaff.
Visiting his parents, probably the last
time. The van door closed. Mike
disappeared with Sadie at his heels.
Her tail wagging in circles until
the backdrop of night swallowed her up.

10.   *Beans*
I entered a coffee shop
in a new town I just moved
to. Behind the counter stood
a blonde banged barista pulling
shots and making tulips. Skin
tight black jeans and a pony
tail like Barbara Eden. My speech
stuttered with every move
of her wrist and half slant smile
shot to a customer grabbing
their morning fix. The smell
of chocolate and hickory
from fresh ground beans
illuminated the black and white
wall cafe. Succulents and baby
ferns lined redwood shelves
on every corner. As the line
moved the usual busy commotion
grew silent. A soft buzz pulsated
from my feet to head. I brought
my coffee outside to get fresh air.
Moments later the barista followed.
Smoke break. *Do you have a light?*
That was the first question my wife
ever asked me.

My secretary is piled with prison letters

hand drawn old English
and Salvador Dali style cursive
I have a hard time reading
        others are almost illegible
           backward *j's* and missing vowels
                important ones are punched
                from an old lap-sized typewriter
                with sultry keys that bleed
                soft soot ink
        they all have the meticulous precision
                              of museum hung calligraphy on canvas

p.o. boxes hang loosely on sticky notes
next to a calendar void of white space
        my pens and bookmarks rest
        in a broken James Joyce
        souvenir mug I picked up
                        in an Oregon bookstore by the ocean

I detail seaside trips in my letters
crossing state lines with ease
        lone trips in the mountains
        and ancient bristlecone pine forests
                      where solitary carries another meaning

the letters are jumbled among
holiday cards and parole recommendations
        they fill up filing cabinets
        next to my side of the bed
                when I dream I can almost hear
                      them read out loud

I make frequent trips to the post office
        they know me by name and labor
I get fancy stamps every month
        I don't care the extra value
                      as long as they bring a little bit of joy

I don't remember holidays for religious reasons
or racist dead president's birthdays
        mail isn't picked up on those days
                      so I plan accordingly

I respond as if I'm writing to myself
or to a father who lost his son
or a brother my mother buried
or to the friend who never made it back
                                    from earning a purple heart

I can still taste the cheap adhesive
I licked while in chains
and I'm afraid if I stop I'll forget
                                    how to spell my own name

Jack's Eternity

I.

I first met Jack at Lunas. Neon
reflected off his freshly cut eight ball.
Shattered vinyl beard parted for the neck of an anchor
steam lager. His finger struck the Pleiades and the sliver of moon
divided his face. He sprinkled rosemary and lavender in cheap pipe tobacco rolled
in thick bugler paper. Chain smoking through performances. A poet would take the
stage and Jack would huddle the corner in soft whispers.
He was shaped like a bull but his iris' held petals. Or hallmark
greetings. Or the scent of a mouse fed to a python. Old
shredded leather jacket hung from him like armor.
His pupils fluttered like pinwheels

caught in an evening draft. I bought
him a beer before he took the stage. I left expectations
in my pocket next to my bicycle lock keys and NA chip.
Jack silenced the cafe. His breath pulled in like ships docking
the harbor. He sat down and smiled. When it was over I gave him my number.
He went north. I went east. I took the long way home across the rail yards and rivers.
At twilight Jack called in paranoia. We met at the city's signature bridge
to watch the sunrise. *I feel like three people* he finally said
and I don't know which one to believe. I had no comment.
I thought about telling a joke but decided it inappropriate.
The sun yolked over the valley and we departed.
Jack rolled a boulder until I could no longer see him.

II.

I filmed Jack climbing a boxcar in Old Town.
My wife threw rocks against wooden planks
while singing Velvet Underground lyrics.

> Somewhere beyond the Sierra Nevada
> weather was unfolding like a back pocket
> postcard. An unknown sender. An unknown
> destination. A place we don't want to forget.

We were documenting the city art scene framed
against mental illness. The only way to navigate
such a painting. Both sustain the other. Jack
paced between the river docks, hand gripped
along his belt loops to keep his pants from falling.

> His large frame twirled like a feather. Effortlessly
> dancing. When he spoke it was as if a lighthouse
> was guiding you to safety. *I don't want others*
> *to feel so alone like me he said.*

At dusk we entered
a cheap roadside diner.
A slice of cheese on top
of pie kinda place.

> My wife ordered pancakes. I ordered coffee. Jack
> quoted the Iliad. He retold the memories
> of his childhood raised in Mormonism.

That's why I'm so fucked up he said *but that's also why I'm such a good artist.*

Jack left for his first date with a man while my wife
and I played sudoku across from the table. The next
morning Jack knocked on my door.

That prick stole my wallet.
Who? I asked. *My date. He trashed*
my apartment and took my heart.

> Jack gripped the door frame with his left hand.
> His right hand stroked his beard. The teapot
> whistled through the hallway and he shook his
> head when offered coffee. Jack rolled a boulder
> until I could no longer see him.

III.

Jack called one morning as I pulled into the job site.
The morning frost arched across the hillside. My breath
catching glass. A welcomed opportunity to climb
an extended ladder without the danger of heat stroke.

> Chickadees conversed behind the window pane. Scrub
> jays gathered the riverbank of the Umpqua. Jack crafted
> paranoia as if polishing dogwood. Something only a poet
> can do. I felt guilty for no longer being neighbors.

For no longer eating garlic noodles at 2 am. For no longer
living in the same town. *Suicide today* he explains. I took
off my painter's belt and sat beneath a canopy of pine wood.
Did you know Nietzsche said you have to die several times

while you are still alive? I told him I didn't. *I wonder
how many times I have died?* He let out a sigh followed by a hacking
sound. I imagined his section 8 building against the levee. The light
rail across the dirt field. Carefree joggers running with dogs along

the bike trail. A father teaching his son how to fish. I missed
 the long nights sitting on his 4th floor patio. I lit a cigarette
so we would at least be smoking together. A trivial connection,
but a connection nonetheless. I'd take all I could get and so would Jack.

His therapist called him and he had to go.

Happy birthday my friend, I love you I said before he hung up.

Jack rolled a boulder until I could no longer hear him.

IV.

For the length of a dream I disappeared
in a deep pocket of white-bark pine,
pacific yew and blue oak. Solitude.
Stream bathing. Silence. When
I returned from the forest I learned
of the murder of 2020. The streets
were occupied with angry bodies.
Sad bodies. Tired bodies. Precincts
taken over. Burning a beautiful soot hue
with a splash of revenant. I knew Jack would
be involved. The city embraced my absence like
a 5x7 lodged inside a 4x6 frame. I bought sandwiches
and met Jack in a southside park. His velvety placid
cheeks no longer carried the skin of salmon.

His left hand scraped raw. His right
hand bruised, stiff armed to hold
him up above the grassy patch.

Like a steel beam kept in place
to keep a tree from leaning. I threw

my shoes off and gave him a flower.
I wish I could remember what kind.
Jack's nose was aquatic. Bent
like the branch of a corkscrew

willow. I asked him what happened. *I had
an episode* he said softly *I was confused
and the cops threw me into solitary for a month.*
An image of Our Lady of Guadalupe thrown into a boiling
cauldron appeared. A newborn doe whimpering in limp
from an amateur hunter's off-target buckshot.
A jagged kidney stone passing through a too small

urethra. We ate the avocado and French
soft rolls with minimal words exchanged.
The trauma hung from his wily grey beard
hair. In the distance two brothers tossed
a frisbee. A young red headed girl smacked
a tether ball round and round a pole protruded
from a used tire. A bicyclist sped by ringing

his handle bell. *I can't get into any trouble
or I get sent back* he continued. Jack explained
the entire story until the tennis court lights flared.
The moon too large for any constellations. Jack rolled
a boulder until I could no longer hear him. I left the prison
at noon and drove the coastline. I waved to Caltrans working
on an earlier landside. I thought of the information I presented
to the guys inside and wondered why I was still there.

The first person I remember having sex with

led me through the labyrinth beneath
the poplars of Cesar Vallejo, like an imprisoned
poet whose blood finally circulates. She had soft
features of Blanca Varela and danced
the *supaypa wasin tusuq* between high Andes

lit candles adorned with lily of the Incas
and superstitious St. Rose of Lima.
At 17 I knew nothing except for walking
midnight streets alone, and her quarter
of a century experience revealed

an unblemished scent of alstroemerias
I had only read about. She carried
me home from a funeral, where her
October earth complexion and Quechua
acorn canvas kept my thoughts

of the dead ambrosian. We lived
in the squalor of dilapidation,
like an adobe haunt of Mexico
City, across from homicide park,
where the late-night shrieks

of bullet-fire and knife-sparks
were drowned from the lavish
of bath water. I had never posed
nude before an angelic statue,
or seen my true nakedness

from the view of another, her
golden eyes like quinoa displaced
my flaws onto her corner shrine
of our lady of Guadalupe—cloak
enshrined chrysanthemums and gladiolus—

reciting the same graveside vigil hymns
across mahogany and jet jasper rosary beads.
Every night I traced her stonework
scars like windows and lost citadels
of sun gods.

On my birthday

I was alone, flying from Denver to Northern
California, or maybe it was from Kenai
to Oklahoma City,
        the trips are getting blurred.

I don't remember the last night my head
rested upon my wife's stomach, her soft hands
gently combing through my hair,
        soothing my dry
        lips and double vision,
        telling me *it'll all be ok*. I met

a man at a Midwest conference who spent
more time in prison than I've been alive, he spoke
of riots and rusted screwdrivers,
        Visine bottle syringes
        and untreated resentments.
        His eyes formed bloodshot

swirls when he said *welcome home brother,* an embrace
        I wasn't ready for. The ice shelves and sierra crestline
from 30,000 ft look like hieroglyphics, lightly traced
        fingers resembling a child's hand, drawn and mailed
to a mother in confinement, correspondence of letters
        and art, their only line of communication. How many birthdays do children
miss while their parents carve stone?

My friend was handcuffed to a hospital gurney
while she gave birth, student interns forcefully examined
her insides, patting
        her knee before exiting the sterile room,
        leaving her chained in convulsions, her child
        strangled from hands in uniform.

31 is an interesting age, almost
        non-existent. My mother
                had two children by 31, a pre-teen and one learning
                to walk. As a child in Japan, her birthdays weren't celebrated,
                      but shared with every girl on a single day out of the year.

Not until arriving in America was the individual day
        recognized. I always think of my mother on my birthday.

She's the reason why I always celebrate by watching a Miyazaki film on the big screen, alone. Curled in the furthest corner back seat. Shoes neatly paired to the side. Slowly throwing oiled kernels on the stained sticky carpet.

EVERYTHING IS KINDLING, EVERYTHING BURNS

The house burns like the cherry embers of a forgotten cigarette

    the forgotten cigarette burns the larynx of an opera singer

The opera singer burns like the jazz hands of Thelonious Monk

    Thelonious Monk burns like a star only visible away from neon

The neon burns like a cityscape skyline scorned with Seagrams highball

    the Seagrams highball burns like a dive bar poet enraptured in his craft

A dive bar poet burns like the high-country bears first salmon kill of the

    season the first kill burns like the first kiss of a long-awaited funeral

The kiss burns like the runaway atop the midnight express

    the runaway burns like the summer solstice sunset below the Ozarks

The sunset burns like early morning fog crisscrossing elk meadows

    the fog burns like a riot encapsulating gated communities

A riot burns like a 6-inch knife sliding back only 4

    a knife burns like the death row inmate meditating on his impermanence

My Wife

My wife is wearing a Joy Division shirt today
    I wish I had a job to quit
    Walk away in style
    Like cowboys into sunsets
    Why do my dreams disappear

My wife is wearing an Ernest Hemingway shirt today
    Tommy Lee claims
    He drank a gallon
    Of Vodka a day
    An argument left
    For Socrates, Confucius
    And Anatoly Karpov
    (he won when
    Fischer defaulted)

My wife is wearing a Cats in Space shirt today
    Why did my best friend die
    Of an aneurysm and why
    Was I dating his brother's Ex-wife, I don't need
    Answers but saying these
    Things out loud helps
    For some reason

My wife is wearing a vintage Rush shirt today
    If I had antlers
    I would be
    Anatomically Incorrect
    But could
    Go to any Party with
    Horse shoes
    And no
    One would Complain

My wife is wearing a Kurt Vonnegut shirt today
    Troubled streams
    Flow up river
    Next to rustic cabin
    Plateau built
    From an old poet
    I haven't met
    But hear of
    In circles
    I stumbled into

My wife is wearing no shirt today
      And this is my cue
      To stop writing
      Whatever transpires
      Into my tattooed digits
      Light those fancy
      Candles my aunt
      Sent for Christmas
      And draw a bath
      That only fits
      One person

3. Keitō 系統

Orizuru

all you need is a single square piece of paper

her soft hands glide across
the underbelly of salmon
the gods dance the volcanic watershed
drifting between Ishikari and Tensho Rivers

fold diagonally in half one side of the paper
fold again along the dotted line
fold the flap back
squash fold the flap down

bare feet trample straw mats
entire village feasts late October
little ones and elders share ceremony
green fields fade cherry blossoms crumble

flip the project over
repeat the last steps then
fold along the dotted line
squash fold this flap down

her palms held to heart
and forehead kisses swept dirt
first season salmon enter through windows
the fire goddess whispers to the spirits

the base is complete
fold the side flap center
crease
unfold

her older siblings are called to uniform
Mongolian oak lose their crimson
bamboo jut snow like a dorsal fin
a red crowned crane eclipses Mt Asahi's setting sun

fold flap from the otherside
center crease unfold
fold top down repeat
crease unfold

the salmon become rose sponged apparitions
rice fields evaporate into state hands the
currents carry bones of crane
Shinto shrines are squat upon

from the crease lift the top flap
petal fold: lift up push in sides along crease
flatten along creases
turn over repeat on otherside

her innocence is disturbed
as an old man's dream
of war planes and kamikaze explosions
her family dispersed like 75mm shell casings

fold side to center
crease unfold fold to otherside
crease unfold
petal fold bird base is now complete

she steps over leper children
wooden sandals sinking in flesh
refuge is found in an outskirt cave
she has never been so hungry

neck and tail begin
top flap fold right to center
then left to center
flip over repeat last steps

she no longer remembers
the soft touch of her mother's cheek
or the scent of sandalwood
her father would burn at the foot of buddha

fold long thin section
first to the right then left
crease
unfold in between

amputated soldiers roam Tokyo disheveled
Sakura snow ghosts in bamboo forests
she prays to the salmon spirit
but only air raid sirens manifest

turn over repeat
thin section folds right up
crease over existing crease unfold repeat left side
crease left up over existing crease

she reaches for shadows of courtship
wilting anemic plum blossoms
line the walkways of evacuation sites
and envelops the massacre howls

inside reverse fold along last creases
scoop paper inside model
along creases flatten everything
repeat inside reverse fold

the air raids stop
she is in dream between mushroom clouds
gliding her hand beneath
the underbelly of salmon

to fold the head
fold long thin section left down
 crease
unfold

the smolder of napalm
thermal flash burns bones dissolve
clothes burnt into skin
the fire goddess takes her hand

turn model over
repeat right side
make inside reverse fold
along creases made in last steps

a solitary patch of red bare crown
olive green horn heavy with chum
ruffled feathers extend v shaped dance
the flight eclipses the radiation setting

head is then folded
inside neck
fold wings down
999 more to go

Desktop Calendar

no mo yama mo yuki ni torarete nanimo nashi

Plains and mountains All enveloped in the snow—
There is nothing else.
—Joso (1661-1704)

steady creek zig zagging
        sharp bend west ornamented larger body of water
flows in winter's drift circumambulating wild lavender field
        and white sprinkled tulips

dusty small island village
        swaying sturdy stilts
on cushion marsh land
        aged white birch moon bridge
arches beyond river mouth
        connected with milk-bleached meadow

kindle pine smoke
        swims between hatched roof
coils across snow-flaked mist
        light doses tumbling
covers entire powdered countryside
        nothing but reflection

sloped bark chipped spruce
        feathered oak frozen
shadows of steller's sea eagles
        float across southern mountain base
cotton balled long-tailed tit
        curled casanova stance

red capped woodpecker
        and blakiston's fish owl
share bent branch sideways tilt
        scouring riparian field mice
tiny tailed snow track trail
        silhouetted in full lunar rising

stars hidden in december's caress
        cradle sleet sheet pasture
elevated range-line shielding zephyr
        sweeping downward silence

bright ephemeral illusion
    an unfolding from emptiness

        Moon and Snow Covered Trees c1900-1910
        Shoun Yamamoto (1870-1965)
        Wood cut on paper

Hotel Life

Larry taught me how to live out of a Motel 6.
Not just one. All of them.
                Northside, southside, west and east.

Living is a stretch. More like nap stations.
We weren't natural disaster refugees, but maybe
we weren't far off.

                My mother liked Larry. He looked like Kimbo
                    Slice but laughed like Duke Ellington.
                He made sure I never slept under a bridge.
                    He was like Too Short with fortune cookie
phrases. I met him as a fry cook
            at a river-docked restaurant.

The one's where the waitresses sing
        and someone's uncle always has a heart attack.
The one's where you have to wear a trash bag doing the dishes
        or you'll have to throw away your clothes after the night shift.
The one's where Narcan comes in handy when you least expect
        it and all the popular deep-fried hushpuppies are sold out.
The one's where George Orwell worked when he was poor
        in Paris. I refer to this time of my life as Down and Out in California.

If you're wondering what the threshold
is in regards to living at a motel,
it's being able to say you've witnessed
an ambulance wheel out a dead body
on multiple occasions.

        I always wondered if some died in the room I was staying in.

                        Motels are like fireflies.
                        Solar flares. A dumpsite
                        your grandfather takes
                        you to in the middle
                        of the night and forbids
                          to ask questions.

Larry once told me *never stay in the same room*
consecutively and always tip your waiter.

There are codes amongst thieves.
No matter what anyone tells you.

        I forgot about the same room business.
            That's how I met Anthony. He and his girlfriend
        followed bible salesmen from Alabama to Colorado.

When they had enough dough
    they landed in the golden state.
It was my second night in room
    36. Anthony was crying outside the door. His girlfriend was paying
    for their hotel room inside
        and he was stuck in the cold.

            We played spades and drank miller
            high life. My mother liked him too.
            A southern prejudice they could both
            relate to. I took Anthony into my
            business to help with their room fees.
            Business is a stretch. More like a 60
            minutes episode.

Which means we played a lot of pool,
rode the train across town and watched
the sunset across the riverbank. The city
was not kind to them. One day he didn't answer
his phone. One day I found the room empty.
One day they were gone.

Dislodged

Last summer my brother and I filled an entire storage
unit. An 8x16 with all our mother's possessions;
grocery store wire racks, Japanese Tupperware,

seaside landscape watercolors framed in burlap
wood. A decade of downsizing. Hoarding. Gentrification.
The facility is tucked beside the railroad tracks

like a lead-weighted rainy-day fund, but I never
was one to abide by the law of gravity. As a teenager
I got us evicted more times than I'd like to admit,

but this move was beyond my control. Tourists
staking claims on renovations. Arriving in the city
like polluted afterthoughts. My mother's apartment

sat across from the best egg rolls in town and cheapest
cigarettes this side of the American River. I smoked
crack for the first time at the intersection of Folsom

Ave and had my last overdose in the small narrow hallway.
That was almost a decade ago. The new owners of the complex
raised the rent so high every tenant moved out. Some

with nowhere to go. Others, like my mother, only found
availability for an 8x16 bedroom. I visit her often. Feeling
guilty, dispossession was my fault.

Marina

I came here to witness my future. The seaside town
where I learned to walk and pedal without training
wheels. Where my older brother rocked the rat tail
and painted brushstrokes like Mr. Miyagi.
Where I watched my cousins swing nunchaku
in ninja suits while I crawled out of strollers.

I came here because the waves sing a different
lullaby up north, here the language is familiar.
Where my grandfather drank every night at the Legion
Hall. Where my grandmother watched Japanese game
shows between kitchen shuffles lost in sukiyaki smoke.
Where my mother used to sneak out to the dunes to drink

Sapporo with the older kids. I came here to learn
of my memories. Where I threw rocks at windows,
shattering along dilapidated military barracks. Where ghosts
in uniform hovered along the deserted commissary.
Where I played with imaginary friends in kimonos
who looked like my mother before she was forced

out of Japan. I came here to witness my future.
Where my father sold illegal substances in parking lots
along Big Sur watering holes. Where my father lived
in rehab while my brother recited his ABCs. Where my father
learned the trade of an electrician and kissed the seashore good-bye.
I came here to swallow the tin cans. Where the saxophone hangs

taut around stable shoulders at Sly McFlys. Where Miles
Davis took the stage at the Monterey Jazz Festival after splitting
with Coltrane. Where the summer sea lion season transforms Pacific
Grove into siren song falsettos. I came here to gain identity. Where
my uncle plays back sumo tournaments while I eat sesame crackers.
Where my grandmother remembers Hokkaido and the dirt roads of Tokyo.

Where I learned why I have to take off my shoes before entering someone's house.

Low n' Slow

    —for Jimmy Santiago Baca

Is the secret to preparing a grilled
cheese sandwich, according
to my wife.

But it's also what Dogen Zenji told me in a dream.

Zenji means *Zen master*.
Ji when used in *shoji*
means *to die* or *to be dead*

Zenji is a title only bestowed
upon the dead, any other time
would be filling one's ego.
A false prophet.
An artificial evocator.
An unfortunate fortune teller.

Never follow a person who calls themselves an expert.
I tried one time while sitting at a prison poker table.

The cards were from your average commissary
playing deck—except for the jack-of-hearts
—a blue chevy impala delicately drawn between
the corner faces.
Convertible top. Two doors and 200 spoke rims.

I'll never forget the details.

Dogen, which may roughly mean *source of the way*,
told me to stay low to the ground, straight posture,
chin slightly in a tilt—to be slow, not in terms of leisurely
or opposite of fast, but unhurried in the sense of *being-time*.

This is a person who at the age of 12 decided
he was going to be a Buddhist monk.

Who was I not to take his advice?
At the age of 12
I lost all my imaginary
friends and slept in motel rooms.

A year later I would be caught in the current of intoxicants
—following a sorcerer selling pigeons to the blind
and calling them doves behind their back.

I stole this advice from my dream

and brought it back to now. I used to sleep

on tatami mats when visiting my grandmother
        —closer to the ground, closer to the source she would say.

I don't know if she ever came across Dogen,
but she does have a painted stone with Bodhidharma,
                      or *Bodaidaruma's*,

face on it that she carried with her from Japan.
Maybe they're one in the same.

Maybe my grandmother is both of them.

Maybe the answers are as simple as preparing a grilled cheese sandwich.

Poem for Tony Gwynn (who is unaware a first-generation Japanese American is named after him because of his all-time broken records with the Padres and quick speed stealing bases)

My older brother named me. Atop Miramar Street
the sun swallowing Fort Ord. Cactus needles
blowing in the Pacific draft. My mother's Irish
setter roaming empty alleyways and sand dunes.

He and her flipping through Beam Clay covered Topps
baseball deck. The last card in the pile: over 1300 runs
scored, 1138 batted in, and 319 stolen bases. A title
my *ani* was to become for me—teaching the skills left
behind from absent fathers.

>   I've never met anyone named Tony who wasn't an Anthony
>   or Antonio. I've also never met one who was Japanese, except
>   for in Murakami lore, a short story which the premise focuses
>   on the peculiar name of our Asian protagonist, Tony Takitani.
>
>   My mother's name is Betty Ann. A common Japanese American
>   name for a daughter of the ancient ways. Perhaps it's the postwar
>   icon Betty Boop—a symbol for migrating women coming to America.
>   It's only fitting my mother has a tattoo of her as a geisha.
>   I know several "aunties" whose full-blooded matriarch

penciled in the hard consonant words on birth certificates.
I'm not sure why because Betty comes from the Hebrew *Elisheba,*
meaning *oath of God* or *God is satisfaction*, the singular will never do,
we are a family of many goddesses and deities. We bow to the waters

and the skies, never just one. If only my mother picked the name—
Haruto or Riku—something to rhyme with my grandmother Aiko,
it would cause less questions of my adolescence. Her name meaning
little loved one or *one of fortune*. A belly rubber of Buddha. Similar
to my meaning in Greek—*flourishing*, or in Latin—*praiseworthy*,

>   although something I will never be, unless my brother meant
>   it because of the exceptionally high bat to ball contact—
>   over 3,000 connections. My last name, Wallin, was changed
>   from Vallin or Valkin somewhere overseas or on a prison island—root word
>
>   meaning valley. An abundance in the Icelandic Viking origins where the sun
>   is a luxury—my father's side full of confetti blonde hair, porcelain skin
>   and nearly invisible eyebrows—traits unknown to me. Except for my Nordic blue

eyes that define my stature as mixed. The characteristics so obscure

waitress told my wife *your family is so lovely* during a reunion gathering—not knowing it was my family she was referencing.

When I Visit My Mother

We always sit across at a table. Lightly battered tempura
plates and shoyu dipped cold soba. Billie Holiday's
Detour Ahead always plays in the background. The table
is no longer the wooden bench of my childhood, but changes
with each restaurant we meet at—she no longer has a place
of her own. She always greets *ohayou gozaimasu* before
launching into her stories—nostalgia of her once favorite daytime

show *Days of Our Lives* or my childhood with her sitting cross
legged around a pit of fire—terrible dates with men who reveal
they're married. Another hip needing replacement. The stubbornness
of her 90-year-old mother. *Be grateful you are married* she says
I am all alone. No matter how many years I hear this comment,
I still don't know how to reply. Instead, I take her to noodle houses
and sushi bars—sense triggers for old recollections of Kyoto, Okinawa

and Mt. Fuji. But most days those are buried deep in the snow
of sorrow. She doesn't believe in depression but belief has nothing
to do with affliction. Whenever tea and dessert get served
the conversation transmutes into lively positivity—our shared
experiences on Mescaline (her favorite medicine), her first-born
granddaughter, or witnessing me turn 30. *When I get my own place
again, I will make you a big pot of Japanese curry,* she says.

I smile and nod—not telling her those dreams will get buried in the snow of sorrow

Junkie

Never go for the visible veins first; you will ruin half your hustles;
this is the long game not the short game; there is no going back;
to survive you gotta be sharp and flexible; the impatient
one's will have little options; find sympathetic doctors in downtown
and suburbs; really exaggerate the back pain, childhood trauma
and chronic fatigue; never go to the same pharmacy twice in the same

month; never rip off someone who gives you a good deal; learn
a trade, by that I mean lock picking, catalytic converter sawing,
ignition starting, department store buybacks, credit card making,
ID stealing; learn to run fast; don't enter a room where the entrance
is the exit; don't nod off on the public transit; don't mix too many benzos
with your shot; build trust within the transient hotel workers; build

trust with the pros on the corner; build trust with the ambitious gang
members, they'll remember you when climbing the ranks; always carry
adrenaline or narcan with you, you never know; don't fall asleep behind
the wheel; follow behind the old timers; don't snitch in jail; keep a diary
of your thoughts; always wear a belt in case you lose your tourniquet;
always carry cotton, if you run out use the filter of your cigarette;

always carry matches as back up when your lighter dies; when the veins
run out that aren't visible, try to get fresh points every time; if you burn
the bridge with your mother, tell her lies; learn from your father but don't
follow him, no one needs a competition; don't get into a relationship
with someone addicted as you; this may seem romantic, but it only gets
in the way of the real muse; she will only be your friend, the junk will

be your lover; find someone to take care of you; remember this is the long game;
when one city is too hot leave; sign up for methadone somewhere new
and spot out your kind; get a job in a kitchen; drugs are abundant in these places;
the workers will understand your frequent breaks; if they don't find work
elsewhere; get a job with ex-convicts doing labor, by this time you will be an ex-con
too; if the job is getting in the way try to get a slight injury for disability benefits;

when that runs out become a journalist; work your own hours, get paid to meet the
dealer on the way to a source; find new sources and hustles from source connections;
don't fall asleep in the newsroom bathroom; frequent the needle exchange and harm
reduction service centers; but don't be holding while going
in, you never know if the palace is being surveillanced; if you get arrested
and have to do straight time clean your system out; write poetry in jail;

when released publish your journal and words, people
are interested in our suffering and misfortune.

When I Visit my Grandmother

She never stops telling me how handsome I am.
                Even with all the tattoos and scars.
I imagine my great-relatives would treat me as yakuza
                and forbid me from the bathhouse.
I'll find out when I meet them somewhere on the Tokaido Road.
                My grandmother, though, is always welcoming
and sweet. Like soft red-bean mochi. Or low simmering curry.
                I remind her of back home—a place I haven't been
yet but can taste plum blossoms when she reaches
                back to those sea-drift memories. She says my eyes

are hers. And we met along a flourishing watershed generations
                ago. Her husband is gone. Her youngest son is gone.
Her oldest son speaks little Japanese to her and eats in his bedroom.
                My cousin left for the Midwest without saying a word—
dinner plate collecting dust on the dining room table, the wooden seat
                still warm. My mother drives from the valley every two
weeks to tend to her like juniper. She recently watched an Amy Tan
                documentary and told me she is starting to understand
her mother—why she was so hard and tedious.
                I wonder if I watch the same documentary

if I'll finally understand *my* mother.
                My grandmother tells me secrets no one else knows.
I'm not sure what to do with them. I'll store them in me as if I'm an aged
                bottle of sake—only to open when the sun is too tired to rise.
Maybe she thinks I'm someone else, even so I'll keep listening to her past
                because someday I'll have to tell her mine.

Fatherly Advice

My father is almost a year sober. At the age
Paul McCartney asks *will you still need me,
will you still feed me?* He has no grey except
for his Alan Watts's goatee peppered like a snow—
drift maple. His heart is healthy and his cholesterol
is normal. Science would call him an anomaly.
He doesn't think he can drop acid anymore.

Those days are behind him, although I've never
seen him check his rearview mirror. Even while
driving on the wrong side of the road. He's fine
with the auditory hallucinations, but the places
6 decades of experience will take him is too much.
We talked recently of the jails we both spent time
in. The same jails. Different jails. He witnessed

a guard tower being built while serving time in one.
I remember that guard tower when I slept in A dorm.
Decades later. It was the hottest summer on record.
I explained the final product. He was lucky
he wasn't followed by a sniper, you never shake
the paranoia. My friend T was serving a life sentence
when he ran into his father on the yard. I think

it was the second time they met. It took every ounce
of T's strength not to react. I don't know what I would
do if I met my father while playing cards in the dayroom.
Politics would keep us separated—whites and others
don't roll. Would we break the rules and share a spread?
Is a father and son's bond stronger than penitentiary
"diplomacy"? At the card table there are only sharks

and fish. Perhaps I'd finally beat him in spades.
In the same phone conversation, my father gave me advice
on buying a new car. *Get a Honda or Toyota*, he said
*personally, I prefer Nissans. You want reliability
with high gas mileage.* I don't know if he'll ever drink
again, but it's a good sign when our criminal convictions
are layered atop fatherly guidance. That's when I know he's trying.

Meditations on the Anti-Asian Spa Shooting

A little pain in my heart just won't let me be
Wake up at restless nights
Lord, and I can't even sleep
—Otis Redding

I.

My *obaachan* is a mirrored reflection
of the woman who was assaulted in San
Francisco's Chinatown. same delicate
frame glazed atop wooden blocks.
Her resiliency and tough skin
would have had her react
the same—surviving two atomic bombs
tenderizes malleable hearts—she
soothes her pain by transmitting recipes
and new year ceremonies to me
as if rubbing aloe vera across radiation.
How many reincarnations must
we go through just to be seen?
We always have our defenses up.

My uncle was given a DUI while riding
his bicycle home from the bar. He ran
a stop sign beneath a midnight moon.
The marina police officers tracked his
every move that night as if patrolling
the parameters of an internment prison
camp. Don't they know pebbles already
disintegrate into sand? He lost his license,
his job and himself to the bottle. Lost the ability
to teach me how to play the minor scale.
If my uncle wasn't Japanese he may still be alive.

My mother moved to the United States
in 1972. she was 12 years old when she
landed outskirts of Atlanta, Georgia.
Back then the casual chink or jap
name-calling was normality. Shoelaces tied
together, backpacks stolen and burned,
rocks hurled as if firing the first battle
shot—crimson-scabbed bowl cuts
and bloody oriental blossom patterned

kimonos—told to keep her head tilted,
eyes gazed beneath the dirt. The
mother tongue must never be spoken
where it isn't wanted. She can no longer
guide me through *tanka* in *kanji*.

blood moon, winter's drift
island memories capsized,
assimilation,
sky-glow evenings shine dirt paths
light incense and sprinkle rice

hello, how are you?
ohayou gozaimasu
the serpent's dual tongue
slithers between the two worlds
who will carry our language?

blossoms withered bone
weeping willows, lotus root
silk kimonos, torn
splintered getas at the door
the setting sun vanishes

II.

Tammy is afraid to leave her house
alone. Her caramelized Laotian complexion
makes her the darkest resident in the pristine
seaside town of Trinidad (a vacation
renter's market atop the harbor). Her
neighbors spy on her feathered steps
through the market. Every time I travel
to the city I bring spices imported from her
homeland as if a stovetop cauldron
could boil folktales like magic. She knew
one of the spa workers killed and isn't taking
any chances. She is used to this fear.

III.

A couple days ago they deported 33
people to Vietnam, a country none

of them knows. You didn't hear
about it because they aren't reporting
on Asian exiles—they are slowly
erasing our presence—luckily my friend
Tan was not on that flight, he has until the end
of the month to file an appeal while pacing
an Aurora, CO ICE detention center.
He's already served 28 years.

Kunlyna's heart is too large to be

contained within 70 square feet.

It bleeds beyond the prison gate,

flowing into discourse communities

who will never know what it's like

to be referenced as *other*, or given

a death sentence as a teenager. His cell

is his monk's chamber—breathing

in his parents' Khmer Rouge, exhaling

compassion and loving-kindness. We

talk every week about Asian plight

and precepts. Our letters are filled

with entering the places that scare us.

He is a living buddha—adorned

in state issued blue cloth.

We don't talk enough about grieving
 the spilled sencha of survivor's guilt,
The broken bamboo *dobin* carried
from the island of sunrises, the kyusu

stamped with Hiroshige's Tokaido
road that fades like cherry in the wind—
the presence of *yūrei, diyu, gwisin,*
bóng ma, ahp and *lasu* surrounds us.
All my childhood friends suffer from existence.
Names carved in stone stuck in the bardo.
Ancestors never given proper funeral rites.
They endlessly chant the triple treasure
without a host. Carrying the deadweight
of ghosts because there's no other home
for final rest.

hyouhakusha
begging bowls, eternity
gone, gone, gone beyond

For Etheridge Knight

I don't know your experience as a Black man in America
But I do know the stereotypes of being the "model" Asian minority
That which I am not because I share your experience of junk withdrawal
                And the familiar scent of a woman leaving
I too had photos of those I loved while incarcerated, not as long as you
But I know what's it's like on the yard and seeing someone come back
                from the infirmary
                no longer the same

I don't know what it's like in a war overseas, just the experience
through generational trauma
You and my grandfather were both medics in Korea, I wonder
if you met, he was a delinquent too
My grandmother was across the Sea of Japan while you were hit
with shrapnel, hers was in her mind

Opiates resurrected me too when I died after my family disintegrated
Poetry resurrected me too when I left prison
        I beat the entire 7 year stretch
        and I owe it to the love of words
        the ability to express the heartache
Your resurrection is something everyone should know,
so I am writing this poem for you
and myself.

Tony Wallin-Sato is a Japanese American who works with formerly and currently incarcerated students at Cal State Long Beach Project Rebound. He is also a lecturer in the Critical Race Gender and Sexuality Studies department at Cal Poly Humboldt and facilitates programming in youth and adult facilities. His chapbook, *Hyouhakusha: Desolate Travels of a Junkie on the Road*, was published through Cold River Press and he is featured in *We Gathered Heat: the Asian American and Pacific Islander Anthology* from Haymarket Books (August 2024). *Bamboo on the Tracks: Sakura Snow and Colt Peacemaker* is his first book of poems and was selected by John Yau for the 2022 Robert Creeley Memorial Award. His second book of poems, *Okaerinasai*, will be published through Wet Cement Press in October 2024. All he wants is to see his community's thoughts, ideas and emotions freely shared and expressed.

www.ingramcontent.com/pod-product-compliance
Lightning Source LLC
Chambersburg PA
CBHW022149180426
43200CB00028BA/433